# Making Progress

*New Women's Voices Series, No. 142*

*poems by*

# Janet Bowdan

*Finishing Line Press*
Georgetown, Kentucky

# Making Progress

*New Women's Voices Series, No. 142*

Copyright © 2018 by Janet Bowdan
ISBN 978-1-63534-537-7 First Edition
All rights reserved under International and Pan-American Copyright Conventions.
No part of this book may be reproduced in any manner whatsoever without written
permission from the publisher, except in the case of brief quotations embodied in
critical articles and reviews.

## ACKNOWLEDGMENTS

I am deeply grateful to the editors and staff of the following journals, websites or anthologies for publishing my work:

*Best American Poetry 2000*, ed. Rita Dove. "The Year."

*Clade Song*. "Mr. Small & the Changing Seasons"

*Colorado Review*. "Circus"

*Common Ground Review*. "I am the house"

*Denver Quarterly*. "The Year"

*Free State Review*. "Cruise," "The Magnetic Mine"

*Pinch*. "Frankenstein, my father, and me"

*Poetry Daily*. "The Year"

*Smartish Pace*. "Wandering: A History of Whiskey"

*Verse*. "Siren"

Publisher: Leah Maines
Editor: Christen Kincaid
Cover Art: Leah Barondes
Author Photo: Shana Sureck Photography
Cover Design: Elizabeth Maines McCleavy

Printed in the USA on acid-free paper.
Order online: www.finishinglinepress.com
       also available on amazon.com

       Author inquiries and mail orders:
       Finishing Line Press
       P. O. Box 1626
       Georgetown, Kentucky 40324
       U. S. A.

# Table of Contents

Sneak ............................................................................................... 1
12,000 Years Ago, a Girl Was Walking around a Cave ..................... 2
Behind the scenes ............................................................................ 4
Rock Creek ...................................................................................... 5
Circus .............................................................................................. 6
Walking on the wall ......................................................................... 7
The Year .......................................................................................... 8
Wandering: A History of Whiskey ................................................... 9
The Imaginary Housewives ........................................................... 10
Origami & Natural Selection ......................................................... 11
Jamie & Rachel in Liza Lou's Kitchen ........................................... 12
Painting: Still Life with Dog .......................................................... 14
Heads Up! ...................................................................................... 16
Nutcracker: Leah Entrances .......................................................... 17
Mr. Small and the Changing Seasons ............................................ 19
I am the house ............................................................................... 20
Crack of Dawn .............................................................................. 21
At the International Spy Museum ................................................. 22
The Magnetic Mine ....................................................................... 23
Wanted: Panopticon, 4 bedrooms, 3 baths .................................... 25
Memory Ward ............................................................................... 26
Somewhere .................................................................................... 27
Siren .............................................................................................. 28
Cruise ............................................................................................ 29
Falcon Cam, U. Mass-Amherst ...................................................... 31
Frankenstein, my father, & me ...................................................... 32

**Sneak**

**write**  See SNEAK.

[ME *writen*, fr. OE *writan* to scratch, draw, engrave, write; akin to OS *writan* to tear, wound, scratch, write, OHG *rizan* to tear, ON *rita* to write on parchment, Goth *writs* stroke, letter, Gk *rhine* file, rasp, Skt *vrana* wound, tear, *vrhati* he tears, plucks; basic meaning: incision, tearing.]

the word disappears some time in early middle English, manages
        to evade the Great Vowel Shift, sneaks back
(and it should have been **snike!** but there is no snike, which may have been
        what really vanished, vamoosed, snuck off, or
        was somewhere struck off, black-listed, exiled)
to show up in early modern English, spontaneously generated
        and teasing us that we cannot trace it.

| | |
|---|---|
| —something like Penicillin | —unlike **write,** |
| growing out of chicken soup | whose coils and changes we could follow |
| the myth goes | through all the contracts and manuscripts |
| Fleming shoved aside | scribed by monks or merchants |
| one day in the lab until | getting progressively easier to read |
| he noticed the fungus and tested it | attuning itself to its own sound or our speech |
| (**eureka!** I have found antibiotics) | until we overlook its past, ominous history: |
| strange then that the attempt | to write is to wound, to inflict, to tear |
| to reproduce original conditions | if nothing else the ground we write on |
| failed, & failed: nothing grew | (*firum foldan, frea almihtig*) we walk on |
| Yet we have penicillin: it must have | destroyed the first story to build a second |
| come from somewhere, a lightning strike | leaving char & smoke behind but also |
| a miracle, a secret shove in the right | direction. |

## One Day 12,000 Years Ago, a Girl Was Walking around a Cave

Coming out of the cave
Everything is so bright!
We are dazzled, stumble
Like at an awards ceremony
Where we're not sure it's our name
They've called, and our neighbors
Have to push us towards the stage
In our 5-inch heels and dramatic, billowy skirts,
Which we trip on—
It's not the best evidence of our achievement,
The ideas we followed out of that cave
Where we lived indolently, comfortably.
Sure, it was limited. But it wasn't all darkness.
Our eyes adapted. We saw phosphorescent animals,
We built labyrinths and palaces, and cities.
It wasn't so bad but it felt
Insubstantial, a shadow of what we could do
Or learn. It wasn't enough to fill our dreams.

You should have seen our paintings
The ideas we followed out of the cave—in fact,
Everyone had different ideas. The painters were looking
For a background and some perspective; one family
Got so mad at each other that they imagined the world
Outside had five different directions and they went out
So each one could get as far as possible from the others,
And four of them did. The fifth came back in saying now
He'd have all the space he wanted. Some looked at the water
Dripping into the cave and wanted to find its source—
They thought the sky was open instead of just an umbrella
Or the roof of the world as obviously it is, they thought
It went all the way up. And some saw the dandelions:
Miniature suns pointed them out. They started farms,
Vast fields of dandelions everywhere so all of us
Could have the leafy greens. Some thought there must
Be something more powerful than the cave, and some

Thought there couldn't be, and they went out arguing
With such concentration that it took the fresh air to make them
Realize they were out. Then, of course, they started looking for proof.

**Behind the scenes**

are more scenes.

The curtain lifts and we see green country,
 a winding road, a little car.

Set the scene: in the car,
you, and because it is your car

it is a convertible, and because
I love you, I am in the passenger seat.

We have just married, just
waved goodbye to everyone

and driven north to Vermont.
The backdrop rises: night, a city,

an airplane. I am next to you
watching the movie. All the characters

are clay figures, but so expressive!
Just the lift of an eyebrow, and we

know what the dog would say, is saying.
Years later, there is a studio fire:

those scenes are lost, but we have the car,
we have the lift of an eyebrow, a laugh.

**Rock Creek**

Outside we cross the street, walk
A few paces downhill, turn left and we are
In the woods on the trail, deep into the heart
Of the country. The trail winds down and around,
Across a road, and then it is full on
Woods, clambering down rocks, trying
To avoid tripping on the roots, balancing
On the stepping stones to get across the creek
And since the path winds, we cross the creek
Four times, finally coming onto the rocks
At the level of the creek and skipping stones
Or trying to. Above us is a path joggers run on,
And above them is a road where the cars cruise by,
And beyond that there's a city where politicians
Play with power, but down here there are rocks
And a creek. The boy throws a rock into the creek,
And his dad says, it took that rock millions of years
To get here, and you just throw it back where it started.

**Circus**

the nightly parade:
animals
slurping fairground foods
at the side shows
heart over heels, cartwheels
turning into the farmyard work
producing gymnastically, joyously.
here's the next crop, the new
generation into each life
a little reigner the heart
falls for, oh sweet, sun engendered
fertile ground, sudden husband,
family and now son and air,
this life from words and music.

**Walking on the wall**

Which wall is this?  the one I see Noah walking up,
graduated steps until it's so high if he fell on the paving stones
the world would end.   I freeze.  And he, perfectly happy, going up
and up, steady and sure-footed, making me wonder
if it's not me, my vertigo kicking in to terrify me with the prospect
of excessive caution I try to keep from limiting anyone else
of disaster of falling of going down
until my husband yells NO, heads there fast to catch Noah startled,
crying, held safe to be yelled at & kept crying in his angry father's arms.
Not just me, then. And the world goes on, in anger and relief.

## The Year

When you did not come for dinner, I ate leftovers for days. When you missed dessert, I finished all the strawberries. When you did not notice me, I walked four miles up hill past you and into Florence and five miles the other way. When you did not like my dress, I wore it with gray silk shoes instead of gold ones. When you did not see my car had sunk into a snowdrift at the turn of your driveway, I took the shovel off your porch and dug myself out. When you sent back my poems, I made them into earrings and wore them to work. When you refused to appear at the reunion, I went to the dentist who showed me X-rays of my teeth. When you did not tell me you would be in town, I met you on Main Street on the way to the library. While you had dinner with me, I walked past the window and looked in. You were not there.

## Wandering: A History of Whiskey

The maps are rolled into a Glenfiddich tube.
Here is the temperate zone, 1651—
    drawne according to ye truest
Defcriptions & beft Obfervations
    Yt have beene made by Englifhe
Or Strangers. I would like to go there.
    Glenfiddich was established in 1887
Already more than 200 years later
    than the map (NEW AND ACCURAT)
Where you can see Scotland. That part
    is quite filled in with names and Earth,
Crowned with castles and holding a horn of plenty,
    lounges nakedly above.
I am sure this connects to whiskey
As surely everything does, how it's made
    with water from highland streams
Or peat bogs—I went on a tour once,
    don't remember what the factory guide said.
But it has been distilled on purpose
    to elevate and drown the sorrows
Evaporates astonishingly fast
    in the right company or wrong
A view of the world warmed by the glass
    it's seen through, expansive at first:
Let us explore vast fields of barley, then reap
    those golden acres, wait as the grain
Sprouts, ripe for the roasting you have already scented.
    The discovery of North Sea oil in the 1970s
Benefited the Scottish economy. Other industries: textiles,
    whiskey, beer, fishing, the Oxford Encyclopedia says.
    It says the massacre at Glencoe by William III
"tarnished enthusiasm for his reign." I should think so.
After, roasting, mashing and distilling. Any trace
    of the original grain in the refined whiskey spirit
Has a print of the earth, what lived there first
& we drink it to get back.

## The Imaginary Housewives

I didn't know how many of them there were.
Obviously Betty Crocker, smiling at me
From the binder of the big cookbook I'd open
And read, making most of the cakes eventually;
Aunt Jemima, another smiling woman always
Encouraging when the batter on the griddle
Threatened to join into one immense pancake
Instead of five neat ones; Chiquita Banana!
Fruit salad on her hat; the Maxwell House woman
Feuding with the Nescafé woman too lazy to make
A real cup of coffee. I didn't know about Mrs Busywoman,
So rushed she didn't have time to cook her family's dinner
But thanks to Quick Frozen Foods she could zap
Something delicious up in no time! Or Mary Meade
Unreal author of a friendly cooking column in the Tribune
For decades—welcomed you into her unreal kitchen,
But in it you'd make just the dishes you needed to entertain;
Or Kay Kellogg, writer of the book of good things
To make and eat (unable to taste her own recipes
Being insubstantial)—let me tell you, once
I made a cheesecake and put it in the oven. The thought,
Did I put the sugar in? occurred to me five minutes later.
No, I hadn't. I took the cake out, poured the cheesecake
Batter off the crust, mixed in the sugar, put it back.
It turned out fine; nobody knew. Until now.

**Origami & Natural Selection**

A plague of locusts litters the room
Half-made, wings folded back,
Wings at an angle, bright colors,
All of us trying to shape the paper
To our will. A square becomes
A triangle, but you have to rip it
Carefully. A triangle becomes a body,
Winged, the white underbelly
Looking like a chrysalis that
The bright wings emerge from.
It's not easy, creation. Some
Things never make it. Some are
Beautiful. These are not the only
Options.

## Jamie & Rachel in Liza Lou's Kitchen

It feels like coming home
only enhanced—like everything really is
easy, like the illustrations:
housewife in heels, shawl-collared dress with
nipped-in waist and A-line skirt
dazzling beholders as she sweeps dust-
bunnies into a pan. The pan is beaded,
the broom bristles and handle and all
are beaded, even the dust-bunnies are beaded
(and shaped like starfish)

into this kitchen dances the newly
engaged NASA intern ready for breakfast.
Cap'n Crunch (beaded) and blueberry
muffins (beaded) await him; this is
a kitchen in full motion, the beaded
water pouring from the beaded faucet
onto the beaded dishes while the mixer
(beaded) is poised above the beaded batter
next to the beaded cookbook, left open at
the cherry pie recipe (the NASA intern can
bake a pie in the blinking of an eye, but his tastes
incline more to eclairs. How the blue berries twinkle!)
We have set a camera on Mars. The NASA
intern looks out through the beaded curtains:
where is she?

Oh, she is outside, laying the red and white
beaded tablecloth on the table in the beaded grass.
A beaded bumblebee sits
on a beaded flower, picking beads of
pollen up with her feet. More and
more beaded flowers will come of this.
Rachel's twinkling toes pirouette through the grass as she sets
beaded plate after plate in its place. Calling Rachel,
he taps on the glass. Barometric pressure is low, indicating shower
Come in, he says, and though she can't hear him, she knows

what he wants, and she comes in. What? she asks him
standing on the beaded tile floor. The pie is in the oven
decorated with the phrase, "women's work is never done," a beaded sigh
of the artist's utter exhaustion, absorption, and finally
complete in this interior, dinner always almost ready.

**Painting: Still Life with Dog**

Left on a train in Italy
In some countries it would be umbrellas
But this is Italy so it's a painting
Still life of fruit with dog
Sold at auction with other lost items
The chance of buying such a thing
Maybe he liked the dog
Or the colors matched the kitchen
Where he put it

With the other painting, a woman
In a garden. It's Turin, 1975, and
The Fiat worker pays $70. Does he think
That's a small fortune at the time, or
Does he come home to tell his wife,
Look! Aren't these just right for
The kitchen? And a bargain! Either he liked
Them (& why else buy them) or they grew
On him, since he took them to Sicily when
He retired there. Only when his son
Sees the still life with dog in an art book
Does he realize it's a Gauguin. And
The woman in white in a green garden
Is a Bonnard, both stolen from London
In 1970.

London is where you lose umbrellas,
Usually, on the train. You don't want to think
Somebody could have taken your umbrella
On purpose. It was a nice umbrella, nicer
Than theirs. They needed an umbrella. They needed
That nice Gauguin, that lovely Bonnard or
They needed that lovely million pounds or lire
But then they fell asleep on the train
And had to rush to get off to make their stop,
Juggling the packages. They took the cheese
Instead of the paintings, maybe, or whatever

Else they'd packed to look legitimate. They took
The umbrella. The original owners have died.
The police are looking for heirs but in default
May return the paintings to the automaker
And his son. Will they put them back
In the kitchen? Once you know something's
Worth that much, is that famous, can you
Enjoy it?

There's the dog, lying patiently
While the painter works, putting layer
After layer of color in the bowl of fruit:
There's the automaker's wife at the kitchen table
Rolling out pasta, cutting it into ravioli,
Mezzelune, capelletti, agnolotti
While the tomato smell of marinara
Fills the kitchen and the automaker's son
Comes in to ask about dinner.

## Heads up!

incoming…this is a day for the wounded, choose what you will, heart or head. Until the 16th century the head was not much attended to, though the ventricles were thought to be where angels played; they were breathed in. Across the field you see Alice and her flamingos at croquet, uncurling their necks and looking 'round when they come too close to the hedgehogs. The game is all very well, but they know enough to protect their tender heads from the spines; they keep their heads while all around the Queen of Hearts is yelling, off! my head hurts: I hear such conflict, see the stubbornness in these faces reflected and refracted, from this room to the building to the street to the block to the city; there may be cities where instead slow smiles begin or joy flowers out suddenly, but we are not hearing of these. It may be that all we need do is keep our eyes open or keep walking and accidentally breathe in angels.

## Nutcracker: Leah Entrances

Years ago, her sister was a reindeer and she wants to be
her own person but catching up the six years between them,
dancing into the space her sister's left.

she's heard the music played
on flat pink disks, Barbie princesses swirling
in looped swaths of ballgown. Her leotard

is pink, pink tights, shoes, cheeks. For contrast
her brown hair swings from its ponytail, her bright eyes
half-closed while she imagines herself on stage
toe heel turn, palm to partner's palm, turn

we make it through a snowstorm, drivers slipping to reach
Clara on stage alone in the middle of the night
it's all been happy crimson velvet and then she hears
squeaking "all around her, a thousand little feet
scampering behind the walls, and a thousand little lights peered out
through the cracks in the woodwork…." "bigger and bigger
bands of them, and in the end they formed ranks," the rats,
" just as Fritz's soldiers did before marching off to war"

her dance: out from under the skirts
of a smiling man children emerge
as if set free. All their steps rehearsed
even the two naughty ones who range further
delay, stall, pretend not to notice the beckoning,
the hands on hips, the command to return
all rebellion choreographed

half of her is white with blue dots, half blue
with white dots.
another dancer drops a hair-ribbon on the stage,
the focal point we are riveted to
until our half white half blue girl
dances back, picks the ribbon up, turns and goes off

gracefully, as if all part of the comedy
everyone applauds

## Mr. Small and the Changing Seasons

Keep your head down—flying objects,
deserved calumnies or not. The whole shebang
goes, shock waves traveling up to shatter
the glass everything was made of
so the blow is from the bottom: it breaks
from the top. We read to the boy over and over again
Mr. Small's Little Auto, how he treats it with such care
pumping up five gallons of gas, the numbers turning
click-click, glug-glug, we add the sound effects, think
of the sticker shock Mr. Small would have 70 years later, think
what *was* a stop-go sign, and did policemen really
have to carry it with them?  that's where we can hide
our heads, in the past, when flying out of it come the mistakes
we still haven't learned from, haven't somehow felt propelled
enough to reduce our reliance on the little autos we learned to love,
going chug chug backwards down the driveway, vroom vroom
on the seat cushions or the tabletops. Will he have a world
like this one? Are we driving full tilt into a wall? Where
are the policemen carrying their stop-go signs, telling us when to stop?

We go outside; the boy climbs onto his scooter & I push
saying be careful, hold on. He climbs off, pushes the scooter
across the snow, finds a puddle and tests it—thin ice. He inquires
and I tell him, yes it's ice over the puddle, already
he's cracking it because it's melting, it's mid-March, it's spring, and he
stomps in the puddle splashing mud about and I think
"mud-luscious"—back then was Just-spring later? Have we
warmed up?  hard to believe with heaps of snow covering
all but the edges of the lawns. Snow melts to water, water freezes
to ice, I slip on it, it melts back to water: reversible change, even to my bruises.
Welcome cycles, the double helix, the coming spring: now raise
your head, look—the trees blossom, the mercury in the glass climbs.

## I am the house

*(for Noah)*

we bring him home two days old
        and out, for family Seders,
        two nights in a row. My mother
says home for him is wherever I am
        and indeed I am, kitchen/dining
room combined, bathroom (all
        facilities, washing, wiping, mess
        out, clean wear in).
I am crib, bed and blanket,
        mirror of moods, music source
        toys and stroller. My father
holds him in one arm, says, he's
        a compact bundle—I too,
first house, home.

**Crack of Dawn**

When we get to the airport, will it be morning? he asks.
It will be 6, the time he gets up, an hour before
the time he's supposed to get up. There are people on the road.
We try to explain that some people—many people—do get up
this early. We are not those people.
But now he's discovered that the sky is light at 10 minutes to 5,
that the third of a moon he sees is lit against a pale blue
and in the east, where we're headed, a lovely pink suffuses the horizon.
He's going to be one of those early risers. He's going to be chirpy.

## At the International Spy Museum

You walk into an elevator which glows blue, then red
As it takes you up to your new mission. "Mission" sounds
more serious when the elevator is rising
and glowing red for danger. You memorize your cover story,
Your new identity. You were 7 but now you are 18, studying art
In England, on vacation in Volgograd. How long? the steely-eyed
Customs guard will ask. Two weeks, you must answer
Without hesitating. You can only see the eyes. Is it your imagination
Or are the eyes squinting, more suspicious? What will you be doing?
Again, you do not hesitate. Sketching! After all, you are an artist.
Mostly you draw guns, and good guys shooting bad guys, but now
You are an international spy at the international spy museum,
You can sketch the site of a potential nuclear missile factory.
You would like to wear a fedora but that might make you look
Suspicious so you refrain. You do try on a pair of sunglasses with
A mustache attached. You do crawl through the ductwork quietly,
Eavesdropping on the enemy. You do manage to find the secret code
And feed it into the machine. You watch a movie reel explaining
The need for secrecy: loose lips sink ships. You daringly tap on the glass
Separating you from the shark tank and jump back when the shark
Slams towards you. You are confronted by the airport official
On your way out of the country. Who did you talk to? You remember
Your contact's name. Will you be coming back to this country? Sure,
You say, and are congratulated. You have maintained your cover
And completed your assignment successfully. You may be recruited
Again for other, important missions.

## The Magnetic Mine

starring Tommy Dorsey and his boys
as they play the Hawaiian war-dance
circa 1942, *Ship Ahoy*. What
makes it Hawaiian? you ask:
why, they're all wearing plastic leis.
The dancer is called into an office, told
she's the only one brave enough
clever enough and ingenious
enough to carry it through; he guarantees
protection—then we see the Japanese agent.

Oh, these silly old films. Easy now
to recognize the cobbled-together patriotism,
the fear or rage or blind bias
that could bring FDR to sign Executive Order 9066,
calling it a military necessity
to imprison Japanese Americans.

Now back to the movie! our heroes,
the real government operatives, show their papers
to the captain, get instant access to all information
on passengers and crew, unlock and explore cabins,
open cases. It is War, you know. If they could bug
the phones they would, but instead the dancer
warns her audience in Morse code, shoes tapping,
and realizing her aim, the receiver writes it out
faster than it's danced—oops.
Maybe we're projecting too much, early guesses
to predict the trajectory our fears take.

Ezra Pound is broadcasting for Mussolini,
radio waves going out: "Well, the Fuehrer,
Adolf Hitler, he did something about it while I
was listening and looking.
There are different degrees
of efficiency." Radio waves coming in,
the U.S. government recording what he says,

May 18, 1942, getting ready for the courtmartial
to come. They'll put him in a cage exposed
to the elements for 3 weeks, waiting
to take him to trial 6 months away.

You could say it rains on the just and the unjust.
You could say collateral damage
but why didn't they bomb the railway lines?
You could say the ends justify the means
or reject it, say better the guilty escape
than the innocent be punished, better
a little gentle mercy. We're back to weighing
a pound of flesh or equally horrifying alternatives.
Where are the dancers?  Where are the plastic leis?

## Wanted: Panopticon, 4 bedrooms, 3 baths

Trying to keep an eye on my child as he and two of the boys up the street and a sister play outside, I realize whoever designed this house in 1890 did not imagine roads, the kind that seem quiet but where cars come speeding around corners; whoever it was decided to plant an acorn by the side of the house, with just room enough for a driveway in between, where the children are now, and he did not imagine that they might play in that narrow area where he put windows too high for me to check on them until they move further away and I can see that they've gotten the hose, turned on the water, totally soaked each other and now are putting on life vests they've taken from the garage, which I couldn't see until this moment, and when I go out they explain that these are not life jackets but jet packs, and they are going to go up, up, up like the oak that towers over this house, shedding rivulets of water as they go.

## Memory Ward

After I type the code to get into the ward (but now they call it Reflections
Care Area), I open the door to see a lady who looks up to see
Me. Oh! She says, looking pleased, as if she has found someone
She knows, someone who'll help her find what she is looking for,
Perhaps the way out through the door I have just carefully closed.

Were you waiting for someone? I ask, & she smiles, shakes her head, "I
Was just looking for" (but here her mouth takes a frustrated twist
and her eyes move into a far-off thinking).
She brings one hand up to the palm
Of the other, the tips of fingers & thumb together, and brushes the tips
On her palm as if writing could bring the word; "I was looking
For," and she shows me a nightlight behind the door, but then that's not it,
She points to a photo next to the door and her fingers tap the girls
In the picture as she counts aloud, "1, 2, 3," but that's not it, she notices
The flowers sewn into my hoodie and brushes them, and I say, embroidery?

Needle and thread? And she smiles—"yes," she says, "that's what I was
Looking for." She has a slightly European accent,
The little elegance added into her speech.
Maybe one of the aides found it, I suggest.
Then I go through the halls to find my mother-in-law, sitting
In the common room at the back of the group.
Let's blow this Popsicle stand, I usually say, but this time
I say, come to lunch with Blair & me?

Yes, she says, & I sign her out & we go.

**Somewhere**

Somewhere there's a leggy blonde humanitarian lawyer
who used to be an actress in indie films
with a cute little curly-headed boy and a bad divorce and
a nanny who might be inclined to divulge too much
to a sympathetic ear
and she's driving MY CAR.
I think I see it sometimes, clean & white & fast-moving,
but then it turns and I see it's a sedan, not a hatchback,
and I just keep driving.

Somewhere (but I know where, because unlike the car
it doesn't move) there's a couple with two cars and a barbecue,
an appreciation for parquet floors and good light,
a fenced-in yard, a preference for bland colors
and a blind belief in vicious lawyers
who tell them they can get triple damages if they sue me
for the lay of the land they ignored until the water came in,
and they're living in MY HOUSE.
I go past it sometimes and hope they love it
but usually I try to avoid seeing it.

Somewhere there's a poet who won the contest
I was a finalist in, and she's published other collections, too,
and has a poet husband and a house big enough for their books
and an academic position with a 2-3 load instead of a 3-4 load,
and is actually really nice, not to mention brilliant,
so I won't hold it against her.

Somewhere there's a bright woman who's given up cooking
But is happy to be taken out to fine restaurants or
to go to dinner parties, witty about the setbacks
In her life (plagues of bugs, attacking whippoorwills), always
Beautifully coiffed and made up, warm and funny,
And I see her sometimes in what's left of my mother-in-law.
Today she hugged my son & said, I miss you so much.

**Siren**

The cars went by sounding like waves and I, spending the night betting against myself, won every time. Every so often a bus would go by and I would be swamped, bobbing, sometimes keeping my head above water, sometimes forgetting or not getting the chance to take a breath before I went under and come up, when I came up, sputtering and sneezing, my hair wet as snakes. It is only to be expected on these nights when the catalpa has finally leafed out and its orchid stars blossomed, crickets rubbing their wings on the rose vine breaking its way through the kitchen screen, and the air itself almost water. A bicyclist with fluorescent plastic tassels trailing from the handlebars, baseball cards flapping in the spokes, pedals fiercely against the sky. Later I find his tire tread pressed into the soft edge of the road and know he leaned into the curve, moving and being moved, out of his need to travel. Sometimes the cars come towards me, white and gold. Sometimes they leave me, red. I waited until the bus stopped outside my window and its passengers, their backs to me, were lit up in the dark. Then I sang to them.

## Cruise

Here's the deal about taking a cruise in this ship, let's say we're in this ship, the Costa Concordia off the coast of Tuscany, imagine the scenery: not on the water itself because that's just Mediterranean, deep blue, blue on the turquoise side, waves and water going up and down, enough if your tendency is to get a little seasick that you'd be happy the ship is really a small town, population 4,000 or so, restaurants, shops, recreation in all shapes and sizes. In fact at that point who cares where you are, cruising alongside all those Italian pasta fields, lemon groves, olive orchards, flat-roofed stucco houses in their various shades of sienna and umber, the colors they name bathroom tiles after back home so you can pretend you're showering in Italy. In fact you aren't close enough to shore to really see it, not until the ship pulls into dock with four or five other towns, all the citizens let loose to roam the narrow streets, bargain with vendors who admire your eyes ("Such blue!") while you ask about the strings of coral, the many cameos carved into delicate layers of shell profiling some ideal beauty whose nose, really, is probably a little too Romanesque if you were to come face to face with her. Cuanto? you ask, hoping it means "How much?" and not "How many?" How much are you willing to pay for this exotic experience, on shore, the chance to explore something foreign and strange and take home souvenirs? You bargain, aiming for a deal before you go back on the huge hotel you're calling home for the moment, spill the bag out on the bed to admire your corals, your shells and then go have dinner at one of the restaurants where, just as you've stuck your fork into pasta freshly tumbled in a rich, red oregano and garlic marinara, there's a thunk and you look around to see who else felt it and whether you should worry. How many others are here having found their sweethearts and celebrating or saved up for this chance to cruise hoping to find a sweetheart or two, or just wanted to see Tuscany without having to worry? And now the ship is listing a little: nobody's telling you what to do but you've seen Titanic and really, that's not where you want to be, stuck down in the hold, so as the pasta slides off the table into a puddle, you head out to the lifeboats wondering if women and children are going first, and if you're going to have to hold on for dear life to something vertical while the ship up-ends. That's when you see the captain, headed ungallantly out to shore in one of the lifeboats, and you realize you're no longer floating in the glow of romance and no such fantasy as pasta fields and you're going to have to get yourself out of the water and on to shore.

**Falcon Cam, U Mass-Amherst**

Mama Falcon's a little dazed
looks up—something's moving underneath
rises up, looks down
it's not the eggs
she's sat on for days,
weeks—
it's something more.
She sits back down, eyes closing,
so tired.
Everybody
could use more sleep.
Eyes pop open.
There it is!  a little chick.
The mama ruffled,
nudges it,
settles back.
Can't settle—up again,
turning around,
on the other side
another chick!  this one
a little fluffier. The mama
tucks it back in, looks
up at the webcam.
Everyone watching
wants to tell her
it's okay, wants to help.
She just has to do it
on her own.

## Frankenstein, my father, and me

Maybe because it's my father
out of surgery out
knocked out & wrapped up in canvas
some material like canvas
who keeps drawing a knee up
despite the meds & tubes &
the loop of excess blood led away
from the repaired heart
that I felt knocked out by a wave
of something like what I shrugged off yesterday
reading *Frankenstein*: the sublime, the mix of horror & awe,
visceral revulsion made queasy by love.
I only got as far as the creation before the surgery.
Here's my father, re-vived, new valve, double bypass,
here's the brilliance of science,
technology, theory, practice brought together
for the best intentions.
Saving life was where Victor wanted to go, too,
and we know what happened to that story.
I had to sit down. The new valve is in the way, stops
the auricles from talking to the ventricles,
they can't get the beat, my father's heart, all our hearts
are like a rhythm band inside us working together,
and if they can't, they find ways to compensate,
and if those adaptations won't work, we turn
to a whole lineage of obsessed scientists who won't let Nature
take its course, thank God, because no one ever has—
we've changed the course of rivers, we've burned off
the fields, we've built factories, so why not create
a pacemaker, implant it, and while we're at it,
there are some cancers I'd like to see obliterated, too,
and if it's chutzpah, it's chutzpah, and I say
go for it.

**Janet Bowdan**'s poems have been published in many journals, including *APR, Crazyhorse, Verse, Gargoyle, Free State Review, Isthmus* and *The Peacock Journal*, as well as the anthologies *Best American Poetry 2000, Poetry Daily* and *Ice Cream Poems*. She teaches English and creative writing at Western New England University, where she also edits *Common Ground Review*. She lives in Northampton, Massachusetts, with her husband, son, and sometimes a lovely stepdaughter or two.

www.ingramcontent.com/pod-product-compliance
Lightning Source LLC
LaVergne TN
LVHW041507070426
835507LV00012B/1389